# Housing, Care and Frailty

## A report on levels of dependency in groups of older people receiving services from Anchor in its' East Pennines Area

Anchor Housing Trust
Anchor House
269a Banbury Road
Oxford OX2 7HU

© Anchor Housing Trust 1990
Anchor House, 269A Banbury Road, Oxford OX2 7HU

Published by Anchor Housing Trust

Printed by RAP Ltd., 201 Spotland Road, Rochdale OL12 7AF.

ISBN 0 948857 46 3

# Anchor Housing

Anchor is the leading charity providing housing and care for older people in England. This housing and care is provided through sheltered housing for rent and special Housing-with-Care for very frail old people. We also organise community initiatives including 'Staying Put' help to older homeowners in difficulties, and look for new ways in which older people can be helped.

Since its work started in 1968, Anchor has built more than 600 sheltered housing schemes throughout England and now has 24,000 tenants. Anchor has its central office in Oxford with regional offices in Altrincham, Bath, Bradford, London and Newcastle-upon-Tyne and eight other local offices.

# The Carpenter Partnership

The services of The Carpenter Partnership are based on the work and research of National Health Service specialists in Geriatric and Psycho-Geriatric medicine who have a particular interest in rehabilitation and community support services.

The aim of the Partnership is to share this experience of the causes, effects and management of mental and physical dependency in old people.

The Partnership was established in 1988 and has accumulated wide experience of local authority and private sheltered housing. Equipped with advanced computing skills and this knowledge of the elderly, it is unique in its ability to understand the problems of providing care and offer effective research techniques for finding solutions.

# List of Tables

Page No

# Appendix 2

# Contents

# I. The Anchor Dependency Survey

This report presents the results of a survey of dependency carried out for Anchor Housing Association. The data was collected between November and December 1989 from residents of Anchor sheltered housing schemes and clients of an Anchor "Staying Put" project.

In the survey, an activity of daily living questionnaire was used to audit the dependency of residents in a sample of Category One and Two sheltered housing, Housing-With-Care and Guardian sheltered housing as well as a sample of past clients of a Staying Put project. The questionnaire was used to take a "snapshot" of dependency as it was discovered in the sample at this particular time.

997 elderly people from Anchor's East Pennines Region were invited to take part in the survey. 840 were successfully interviewed by fieldworkers.

Because the survey looked closely at the physical and mental ability of clients, it was carried out by the Carpenter Partnership, who retain all details about the individuals interviewed. In this way respondents could be assured of the confidentiality of their contribution.

# 2.   Dependency: a definition

Deterioration in the ability to function in activities of normal daily life is often a manifestation of disease. Reduced activity may lead to further deterioration of function, followed by complications from the disease and increased dependency on the help of others.

The effect that a set of disabilities has on making a person dependent on the care of others has been termed their 'relative dependency'. It is therefore more useful than simple diagnosis of illness because it provides a measure of the relationship between disability and the demand for care, both personal and environmental.

Measurement of the ability to perform basic activities of daily living with other measures of dependency, both mental and physical, provides useful information for understanding the needs of older people.

# 3.   The Context for this Study

For those involved in thinking about the needs of older people awareness has been growing that the provision of housing and of care services must be considered together. The adequacy of a package of care services may stand or fall by the suitability of the housing into which it is delivered. Similarly, the viability of a housing solution may well depend upon the availability of suitable care arrangements. When taken with the clear demographic trend within the retired population, this truism has considerable consequences for housing providers such as Anchor. In particular it offers a challenge to those who see their role as more than that of mere landlords.

As the largest voluntary sector provider of housing and care services for older people in England, Anchor offers a range of responses to this challenge. A substantial part of Anchor's response is to be seen in the provision of specialised housing for older people. However, specialised accommodation can only provide for a minority of the retired population. Over the past ten years, Anchor has also developed a range of services for older people who live in general housing.

The Anchor Group houses some twenty-four thousand elderly people in sheltered housing for rent and, through Guardian Housing Association, it is responsible for some five thousand older people in leasehold sheltered housing. As a provider of sheltered housing on such a substantial scale, Anchor is well placed to recognise both the limitations and the potential of this form of housing in meeting the needs of older people. It certainly is not, as some in recent years seemed to imply, a universal panacea for the housing difficulties faced by older people. Nor is it the inappropriate and expensive irrelevance that others have represented it as being. Sheltered housing is one of a range of options which ought to be open to older people. It is, and will remain, a minority provision but one which may have increasing importance as its role within the range of provision to be made for elderly people is re-defined. In considering the future of sheltered housing, two factors seem to lead to the same conclusion: All providers of sheltered housing are witnessing an ageing of their tenant population. For those, like Anchor, who have adopted a "need-based" allocation procedure this process can only accelerate. At the same time emerging patterns for care in the community suggest that the role of sheltered housing needs to be re-shaped to provide for higher levels of dependency than in the past. In this situation the notion of a "balanced community" is no longer sustainable.

This will have far reaching consequences for the nature of the communities housed in sheltered accommodation and for the pattern of services they receive. The traditional role for wardens for the "good neighbour" is only viable in a situation of negligible median levels of dependency. Increasing levels of dependency through revised allocation procedures and an ageing resident population are already exerting a powerful influence upon the role and professional aspirations of the warden.

The needs of some older people will be most appropriately met in the context of more specialised accommodation where a package of facilities and services are available to them. In its innovative Housing-with-Care schemes, Anchor has sought to provide residential care which is developed from a housing perspective.

The design of these schemes begins from the premise of providing a home, with the independence, dignity and security that implies. Into that home a pattern of domestic support and personal care services will be delivered which are matched to the needs of the individual resident. Anchor currently provides residential care for some thousand older people in its Housing-with-Care schemes.

Anchor's subsidiary, Guardian Housing Association, has been a major force in the development of a sheltered housing for sale. Guardian's own developments have been aimed predominantly at those owner-occupiers whose ability to purchase sheltered housing from private sector developers has been limited. Residents of such leasehold sheltered housing often have clear ideas about the level of service they wish to receive, and to pay for! In some circumstances there may be a conflict of interest between those frailer residents who wish a high level of support to be available in the scheme and those fitter residents who wish to limit the consequences for their service charge.

he difficulties experienced by commercial developers of sheltered ousing for sale in the current downturn in the housing market have demonstrated that the development, as well as the management, of such stock calls for a closer knowledge of the circumstances, assumptions and motivating factors of prospective purchasers. As both real and perceived levels of dependency in prospective purchasers seem to be a significant factor in precipitating their decision to buy information in this area is clearly important to both developers and managers of such schemes.

It is more than ten years since Anchor Housing Trust launched its pioneering "Staying Put" initiative to assist elderly owner-occupiers in coping with the problems of effecting repairs, improvements or adaptations to their home. Anchor offers this service through a growing network of local projects, some financed through its own charitable funds, some with grants from central government and the majority with funding from local authorities. Each project, through a team of, typically, three people provides financial, technical and pastoral advice and support to achieve a "packaged" solution for the unique problems of each client. The approach has sought to address the problems of securing improvements and repairs through a recognition of the importance of the circumstances and wishes of the individual.

Although often taking many months from initial referral to completion of building works the Staying Put process is effectively a single intervention to assist the elderly client. Whilst the project staff will seek to tackle a very wide range of financial, welfare rights and other issues for the client they do not offer an open ended support service. The improvement of their property may meet only part of the circumstances of the individual older person and a range of other help and advice may be needed to secure their independence in their renewed home. Through a range of new initiatives Anchor is seeking to explore these further challenges.

Anchor is moving toward a situation in which it is able to offer a wide range of housing and care services to older people. This may encompass personal care and "staying put" services for older people living in their own homes, through the provision of sheltered housing to residential and nursing care. This is not to say that Anchor expects to offer all these services in every place, indeed some are still part of experimental programmes and it may not be possible to incorporate them into the mainstream of Anchor's activity. The frailty of those whom Anchor is seeking to serve is obviously a crucial factor in developing and maintaining such a range of services.

Anchor is committed to providing an appropriate level of support in the circumstances of each individual, and that means not too much as well as not too little. In such fine tuning an accurate picture of the nature and level of dependency in those we are seeking to assist will be vital.

It was for this reason that Anchor commissioned the Carpenter Partnership to carry out this brief study. The research took groups of older people who were receiving one of the main services provided by Anchor (Sheltered Housing for sale or rent, Housing-with-Care and Staying Put) and applied a standard questionnaire to gather information about dependency levels. We hope that this study will provide the basis for further work within Anchor and will stimulate wider discussion of the issues it raises.

# 4. The Elderly Population – Trends and Perspectives

In recent years, interest in the consequences of a rapidly ageing population and the impact of this upon the shape of both public and private provision of services has come sharply into focus. The effects of such changes increasingly impinge on all of us - we all have contact with ageing parents, grandparents and friends and the response of each one of us will shape the pattern of services into the next century. The thrust of this report focuses on levels of dependence within a sample population. The purpose of this chapter is to provide the context of the broader pattern of trends within the population and the levels of services to respond to these demographic changes.

## An ageing population

The population structure has changed dramatically over the past century and is likely to face greater changes over the next twenty to thirty years. It is not only the increase in the numbers of elderly people that is crucial, but more importantly the balance of the population structure as a whole. There are a number of broad trends:

● there are more elderly people as a proportion of the population structure. The proportion will grow more rapidly than any other age group.

● there has been a fall in fertility rates, in England and Wales. Between 1965 and 1985 fertility rates fell from 2.85 to 1.78 births per woman.

● life expectations are higher through improved health and diet, and as a consequence mortality rates are lower. Mortality rates remain noticeably higher for men than women. Life expectancy at 60 for women is a further 20 years, for men a further 16 years.

- there will be a decline in the working population over the next 20 years as the UK's population grows at a slower rate.

- the number of school leavers will fall over the next decade — the 16 — 19 year old age group will fall from 3.5 to 2.9 million between 1988 and 2001.

- the overall numbers of elderly people will grow, but at a slower rate. The balance will shift markedly. By 2001 there will be 5% fewer people aged between 65 and 74, 3% more people between 75 and 84, but the number of over 85's will grow by 47%. By 2001 there will be around 1.1 million people over 85.

These changes in demography point towards an older population, likely to demand a higher level of supportive care from a working population which will form a smaller proportion of the whole.

The changing distribution of the population as a whole in Britain has been reflected in the changing shape of Anchor's own tenant population in sheltered housing. Anchor now houses over 24,000 tenants and these tenants are increasing in age, both on entry date to a scheme and on departure from a scheme. A number of indications illustrate the changes:

- Women continue to outnumber men in old age and this is reflected on Anchor's composition of new tenants in 1989-90: 71% were female and 29% were male. For the whole tenant population the trend is even more marked: 74% female and 26% male. In the wider population, the figures for persons of pensionable age are 66% female and 34% male.

- Living alone is also a pattern in sheltered housing which mirrors the elderly population as a whole — 69% of Anchor tenants live alone, the vast majority being women. Lone pensioner householders in society as a whole, account for 59% of the retired population.

- The population in Anchor's sheltered housing has also aged. Since 1982 the average age of tenants has grown from 75.9 to 78.3 years in 1990. Such an ageing process is likely to continue. In March 1990, 20% of the tenant population was over 85; most recent census information indicates this group makes up 7% of the over 65s.

- Reasons for leaving sheltered housing are illuminating; significant proportion leave to go to accommodation providing greater levels of care. While death accounted for 43% of terminations of tenancy in the year to March 1990, a significant 35% left to enter residential or hospital care. This has been a growing trend over the past seven years.

## Health and disability

While generalisations about health are always dangerous, on the whole poorer health increases with growing age. However it is measured, elderly people are more likely to have long-standing illnesses, be less mobile and to exert a growing demand on all types of medical services. A number of indicators illustrate the extent of the draw on health service provision:

● problems of hearing and sight are likely to see little change when people are in their 60s and 70s, but an accelerated pattern of problems occurs among people in their 80s and 90s. These have considerable impact on the abilities of people to remain fully independent

● elderly people are more likely to have long-standing illnesses and so draw on the services of GPs and hospital admissions. In 1988, the proportion of total NHS expenditure on people over 65 was 49%.

● while women have greater life expectancy than men, they are also likely to suffer the highest levels of serious illnesses and disabling diseases.

Two recent reports by the OPCS on the Prevalence of Disability identified a high proportion of elderly people having some forms of disability which restricted their ability to live a fully independent life. It focused on disability being a restriction of the ability to perform everyday activities, through either physical or mental impairment. The main findings were:

● of the 6 million people identified as having a disability, 4.2 million were elderly people. The vast majority (90%) lived in general non-specialist housing

● people over 80 were more likely to have some form of disability — 75% of this age group

● elderly people are likely to have the severest disabilities of any age group.

• elderly women are more likely to suffer disabilities than elderly men.

• problems of locomotion, personal care and hearing presented the most common problems restricting independent living.

The 1985 General Household Survey results when related to the estimated population, produce alarming figures on the shape of health and disability indicators for people aged over 65:

• 1,088,000 people cannot walk on their own down the road; 670,000 of these could not manage at all to walk down the road.

• 753,000 people are unable to manage stairs on their own

• 167,000 people are unable to get in and out of bed on their own

## The role of carers

The family still remains the main source of support and care for elderly people. However, this is modified by three trends:

• larger numbers of women are working and this trend will continue through the 1990s. Labour shortages are demanding women to become the major component of the workforce. Traditionally the task of caring has fallen on middle-aged or elderly children, usually daughters. Such informal care is likely to be weakened partly through a decline in the 45 — 60 age group, but also due to larger numbers of women in this age group remaining in employment and so are unable to provide the same levels of informal care.

• geographical mobility of employment and residence has also meant families have become separated at greater distances around the country. Traditional support networks are being slowly but surely broken down. Areas of high population mobility are likely to have weakest family links.

• such a decline in the traditional carer comes at a time when statutory and voluntary services are finding it increasingly hard to recruit care staff. This in part reflects low salary levels and also a decline in the number of school leavers — the traditional pool of people to be employed in nursing and care services.

Who are the carers? The 1985 General Household survey looked at the numbers and characteristics of carers;

- 6 million carers in Britain; 1.7 million caring for someone in the same household.

- 3.5 million carers are women; 2.5 millions carers are men.

- Chances of being a carer increases with age.

- 20% of carers look after more than one person.

- 75% of carers look after someone over the age of 65.

## Overview

This discussion has aimed to give some background to the changing demographic and social trends within Britain today. Much discussion has focused on the so-called 'demographic time-bomb' presenting a gloomy picture of the changes ahead.

This need not be the case. Certainly the population is ageing and consequently problems of poor health, mobility and growing levels of disability are to increase. However, the challenge is to demonstrate how proper provision of support services can promote **ability** and **independence** in spite of these changing forces.

# 5. Introduction to Dependency Survey*

In all European countries there has been and still is a decline in both fertility and mortality with a resulting low population growth and increase in expected life span. These changes, though to a lesser degree, are expected to continue for the next four or five decades and this will have an impact on the age structure of the population. Persons aged 80 and over will constitute the fastest growing group among the elderly.

As life expectancy of the female population is greater, there is a considerable sex imbalance amongst the elderly, an imbalance which increases with age.

There is a tendency for older people to live alone. Due to the fact that women live longer than men and given the higher prevalence of widowhood amongst older women, the proportion of single persons is much higher among women.

The proportion of older people living in nursing homes and sheltered housing is surprisingly low. It is not until after the age of 80-85 that institutional care starts to increase rapidly. One reason for this is that despite the high proportion of people living alone, contact with the family seems to be good throughout the years.

Although life expectancy has increased, epidemiological studies have shown a strong prevalence of chronic disorders among older people. As many of these degenerative disorders are not fatal, their prevalence increases with age. The majority of older people, however, are not disabled and can manage without outside help.

The Council of Europe, European Health Committee, in examining screening and surveillance techniques in the elderly in 1988[1], said

---

*Extensively quoted from surveillence and screening techniques for the elderly, Council of Europe.[1]

that voluntary organisations should be stimulated "to play a greater role in encouraging elderly people to be socially active, providing them with information and encouraging them to visit their General Practitioners and other relevant health officials".

Government policy has been increasingly directed towards "care in the community" with the emphasis on keeping older people at home. Before these concepts are implemented there is a need to know how older people are managing to cope in their every day lives and the effect that disability has.

The object of this survey was to discover the extent of disability and dependency of the people catered for in different types of housing initiatives provided by Anchor Housing Association. The survey also collected data on the prevalance of depression in the sample; an area which may be especially significant because of the relationship with dependency.

## Sheltered Housing and Dependency

Opponents of sheltered housing claim that by concentrating older people together in specialised housing, an unnecessary burden of care is placed on the community services, in the "care consumes care" argument.

Proponents of sheltered housing suggest that ageing with like minded and similarly able people enables older people to adjust better to the ageing process and provides companionship and support.

The perceived idea of old age is of frailty and the need for physical aids and services. For the majority of older people this is not the case. Certainly, those that shuffle and use sticks or walking frames may be old, but they are noticeable because of their disability, not because of their age.

Similarly, there may be ideas about sheltered housing which are false, for example, is it true that dependency increases with duration of tenancy in sheltered housing schemes, and are all the oldest tenants in the oldest housing schemes?

None of these arguments can be satisfactorily resolved without establishing some sort of base line for the disability catered for or present in sheltered housing.

The survey examined the demographic characteristics of all the people in the sample and examined dependency in the different categories of housing, paying particular attention to the relationships between age, duration of tenancy and dependency in Anchor sheltered housing. The survey also collected data on symptoms of depression to form an impression of its prevalence.

## Background to the Project

The survey was based on the methodology of a three year study of over 75's from two general practices in Andover, Hants, by Demopoulos and Carpenter[2,3]. The Andover study tested the benefits of regular surveillance of the elderly at home using an activities of daily living questionnaire administered by unskilled volunteers.

In the Andover study elderly people were visited regularly (every six months) by a volunteer, who completed the questionnaire. Individuals with a significantly increased score were referred to the General Practice, requests for aids etc, were dealt with by the research assistant.

This project demonstrated that regular visiting of old people at home by non-professional volunteers completing a simple activities of daily living questionnaire is inexpensive, practical, and has a positive impact on the population visited.

The group not visited regularly spent 33% more days in institutions, most of these long term admissions to residential accommodation. The group visited regularly received community support services sooner and admissions were more likely to be to hospitals than were admissions in the control group.

The Andover study was extended in 1989 to cover depression and is currently being used in a study in sheltered housing in Winchester Health District.

The role of dependency surveillance, screening and other health promotion programmes and activities are extensively discussed in "All of Us, Strategies for Health Promotion with Older People", published by Wessex Regional Health Authority[4].

# 6.  Major Findings & Recommendations

## Major Findings

1.  The majority of tenants of Anchor sheltered housing in the sample were able to cope with everyday activities of daily living and were not significantly disabled by these disorders. In this they were found to be no different from the general elderly population.

2.  Tenants entering Anchor sheltered housing appear to be progressively older. As a corollary, they were also more likely to be female and living alone.

3.  In the East Pennines Region of Anchor Housing, the sheltered housing schemes were uniformly low in overall dependency. No relationship was demonstrated between duration of tenancy and dependency. This uniformity has not been demonstrated in similar studies.

4.  New owners of Guardian Housing are noticeably older, and reflect the ageing population profile, being mainly widowed women.

5.  Residents of Anchor's Housing-with-Care were found to have some or significant disability or were very old. However, this category, because of increased age and dependency, are the most likely to be suffering from undiagnosed and untreated depressive illness. The mean duration of tenancy was low, only 1.8 yrs even in the oldest schemes.

7.  Clients of Anchor's Staying Put project were younger than tenants of sheltered housing, but share the same average level of dependency. They were the least likely category to live alone. Very

few clients aged over 80 had been helped by the project. Staying Put clients had the second highest likelihood of depressive illness, this feature may actually reflect high anxiety rather than depression.

## Recommendations

1.  Investigate further the prevalence and effects on dependency of depressive illness and its effects on resident management in Housing-with-Care.

2.  Explore the benefits of extending the scope of Staying Put schemes using volunteers to administer an activity of daily living questionnaire, such as the Winchester Disability Rating Scale-2, as a screening tool.

    The benefits of regular low level support in previous studies were shown to include structured visiting, the faster provision of aids to daily living and community support services, and lower admission rates to institutions.

3.  Repeat the snapshot of dependency in other regions and at intervals over time since the present study gives no indication of whether the pattern of disability is peculiar to the East Pennines region, a largely urban population, or whether it is stable or changing.

# 7. Methodology

## Sample

The survey was designed to provide an audit of the dependency of a representative sample of residents of three types of sheltered housing, and clients of a Staying Put project in Anchor's East Pennines region.

## Sheltered Housing

The target population was all residents of 22 Anchor housing schemes built between 1973 and 1989, located in seven towns and cities. The survey aimed to interview 20% of residents in Category One and Category Two sheltered housing and Housing-with-Care. These can be described briefly as follows:

*Category One* sheltered housing may or may not have resident wardens and does not normally have communal facilities such as sitting rooms and laundry facilities.

*Category Two* sheltered housing has resident wardens and communal facilities such as sitting rooms and laundry facilities.

*Housing-with-Care* schemes are registered with the local authority as residential homes, but unlike most homes for the elderly, each resident has his own flatlet; meals and personal help are provided.

The schemes selected were geographically clustered to make interviewing less costly, and to have a good distribution of scheme size and age.

In practice, the differences between Category One and Category Two sheltered housing were not clear cut in all cases, and a third category,

'Category One and Two' was introduced. By introducing this category a good spread of scheme age, size and geographical location was achieved. (Table 1 and Appendix 2, Tables A & B)

## Guardian Housing

A fourth category, 'Guardian Housing' was also introduced into the sample to give information on the dependency of its residents. Guardian Housing Association Limited was set up by Anchor to provide private retirement housing, its residents are owner occupiers rather than tenants.

## Staying Put

Staying Put is a project run by Anchor Housing Trust to help elderly home owners who have problems with their property. It helps with advice in all aspects of refurbishing houses.

The survey aimed to interview a representative sample of clients of a Staying Put scheme at an acceptable cost. A sample of 142 past clients from the Hull Staying Put project were invited to take part in the survey. The interviews were carried out on 100 consecutive households giving a final sample of 107 individuals and included husband and wife from the same address.

The distribution of the sample by category of housing is shown in Table 1

**TABLE I Number of dwellings and numbers of individuals by category of housing**

| Number | Cat I | Cat I & 2 | Cat 2 | H-w-C | Guardian | Staying Put | Total |
|---|---|---|---|---|---|---|---|
| Number of Dwellings | 78 | 186 | 281 | 115 | 92 | 112 | 864 |
| Number of Residents | 110 | 219 | 316 | 109 | 103 | 140 | 997 |
| Number Surveyed | 87 | 190 | 277 | 101 | 78 | 107 | 840 |
| % of sample | 10 | 23 | 33 | 12 | 9 | 13 | 100 |

# The Questionnaire

The questionnaire used for the study was the Winchester Disability Rating Scale-2 (WDRS-2). It is a scored 18 item activity of daily living (ADL) rating scale which includes questions about special senses, social circumstance, carers and home conditions. Four items within it combine to give a score which give an indication of the prevalence of depression. Originally designed to record reported abilities in ADL, it can be completed in 5-10 minutes and can be used by non-skilled personnel with the minimum of training.

A full account of the WDRS is given in Appendix 1.

In the survey it proved simple to administer and was well received by the respondents. The results from the questionnaire were analysed by computer using the Depscore programme.

# 8. Dependency Groups

The Winchester Disability Rating Scale-2 generates two scores from the addition of all the question responses, which are scored 1 to 5. The first is the disability score, the second is the depression score.

## Disability Score

During the development of the WDRS three disability groups were defined. Identifying these groups is helpful in itself, but they are also useful for making comparisons.

The three disability groups are:

| | | |
|---|---|---|
| no significant disability | — | score 15-20 |
| some disability but life not significantly impaired | — | score 21-33 |
| significant disability | — | score > 33 |

Previous experience has shown, for example, that it requires only a few people in a sheltered housing scheme with significant disability to generate a markedly increased burden on a warden. The burden on the warden may seem out of proportion to the number of people who have this degree of disability.

Many older people have some impairment of hearing and experience disturbed nights, these two are features of all three disability groups. Other representative features of the disability groups are broadly described as follows:

## No Disability

Older people with no disability can go out independently, have no trouble with looking after themselves and eat normally. They would not normally be confused or anxious. This does not necessarily mean that they have no medical illness. It means that any illness they do have does not significantly interfere with their ability to live independently, and they probably require little or no help.

## Some Disability

People with "some disability" will still be fairly independent but will have problems in some activities of daily living; this may mean that they are no longer able to go out independently or have a bath. Because of the decrease in function they are more likely to need help from the Home Help service or Meals on Wheels. Since the risk of becoming depressed is related to dependency they are more likely to be anxious and weepy, having headaches more often and more problems with sleeping at night. They may have active acute illness, but equally they may simply have a degree of disability that is stable.

## Significant Disability

Typically, people with significant disability are usually housebound or chair or bedfast. They may have difficulty undressing and washing and are unlikely to manage a bath on their own. They may have more severe problems with hearing and sight. Sleep patterns may be disturbed to the extent that the person is very confused, disorientated and awake by night and asleep by day. They are likely to have one or more medical conditions, either acute or chronic, that are the cause of their disability.

## Depression Score

A person scoring more than 8 points from the four depression questions, has a 75% chance of suffering from depressive illness. 15 — 25% of the general population aged over 75 suffer from depressive illness, a factor which is likely to increase their relative dependency.

Depression may only be manifest as a decrease in function rather than a recognisable mood change. The individual who has difficulty eating, dressing and bathing, yet is not depressed and is socially active, is very different from a person with equivalent disabilities who is depressed and isolated. As depression is a treatable illness, clearly, identification of those who are depressed is desirable.

# 9. Fieldwork

## Advance letters

Anchor East Pennines Regional office prepared and delivered an advance letter to each of the residents in the 22 selected Anchor housing schemes. For the Staying Put project, interviewers posted letters to clients a few days before they were ready to interview. Respondents who were not willing to take part were asked to inform their warden or regional office. A few did this and interviewers were informed.

## Interviewers

Interviewers were recruited by a Fieldwork Company, who select, train and supervise all their fieldworkers. Fourteen interviewers worked on the survey, taking large schemes in pairs and working on their own for small schemes and the Staying Put project.

## Briefing

Because the WDRS-2 requires minimal training the fieldwork supervisor was briefed on the use of the questionnaire and the fieldworkers given written notes.

In addition, wardens from the selected schemes and Anchor regional staff, were asked to attend a briefing session where the purpose of the survey was explained and the questionnaire itself studied. This proved to be of great benefit as respondents could receive an informed response to any questions they had. In particular, wardens were able to reassure respondents on the importance and confidentiality of the survey.

Following the briefing meetings, (one in Leeds and one in Nottingham)

Anchor staff were generally very enthusiastic about the project and contributed significantly to its success.

# Fieldwork dates

A set of preliminary interviews was carried out in two Anchor Housing schemes in Chesterfield; one sheltered housing and one Housing-with-Care, to check the efficacy of the advance letter and the number of achievable interviews per day.

These interviews were supervised directly by the Carpenter Partnership. Interviewing started immediately afterwards on December 7th and was completed in January 1990.

Because of the 'flu' epidemic in late December 1989, schemes with a significant number of sick residents were revisited in January 1990.

# 10. Findings

## Location and size of schemes

The sample was drawn from a wide range of towns and cities in the East Pennines region (Table 2) and from schemes of varying size, (10-79 places) and age (completed between 1973 and 1989).(Appendix 2 Tables A&B)

**TABLE 2** Location of scheme by category of scheme

| Location | Cat I | Cat I & 2 | Cat 2 | H-w-C | Guardian | Total |
|---|---|---|---|---|---|---|
| Chesterfield | | | I | I | | 2 |
| Bradford | | 2 | 3 | I | | 6 |
| Shipley | | | I | I | | 2 |
| Nottingham | I | I | | | | 2 |
| Halifax | 2 | | I | | | 3 |
| Leeds | | | 2 | I | 2 | 5 |
| W Bridgford | | | 2 | | | 2 |
| Total | 3 | 3 | 9 | 4 | 3 | 22 |

## Response Rate

Eight hundred and forty interviews were achieved from the sample giving an overall response rate of 84%. This was composed of 729 interviews from Anchor sheltered housing and 107 from the Staying Put project. Response rates for individual categories are shown in Table 3.

**TABLE 3 Response rate by category of scheme**

| Number | Cat 1 | Cat 1 & 2 | Cat 2 | H-w-C | Guardian | Staying Put | Total |
|---|---|---|---|---|---|---|---|
| Residents | 110 | 219 | 316 | 109 | 103 | 142 | 999 |
| Interviews | 87 | 190 | 277 | 101 | 78 | 107 | 840 |
| Response Rate | 79% | 87% | 88% | 93% | 76% | 73%* | 84%* |

* Because interviews were terminated once the target had been achieved the true response rate is marginally higher.

# Age, Sex and Marital Status

The average age of the sample population is 77.9 yrs, with a range from 44 to 104. 15% are under 70 and 23% are aged over 85. Women form 75% of the total sample with a range of 67% of the under 75's to 82% of the over 85's (Table 4).

30% of the population is composed of married couples, 49% are widowed women. The majority (55%) of the men are married compared with only 20% of the women. The ratio of widowed women to widowed men is 5.5:1 (Table 5).

**TABLE 4 Age and sex distribution of sample**

| Sex | >70 yrs | 70-74 yrs | 75-79 yrs | 80-84 yrs | 85+ | Total |
|---|---|---|---|---|---|---|
| Male | 36 | 54 | 63 | 35 | 35 | 223 |
| % age group | 29 | 37 | 28 | 23 | 18 | 27 |
| % sample | 4 | 6 | 8 | 4 | 4 | |
| Female | 90 | 94 | 160 | 118 | 155 | 617 |
| % age group | 71 | 63 | 72 | 77 | 82 | 73 |
| % sample | 11 | 11 | 19 | 14 | 19 | |
| Total | 126 | 148 | 223 | 153 | 190 | 840 |
| % age group | 100 | 100 | 100 | 100 | 100 | 100 |
| % sample | 15 | 18 | 26 | 18 | 23 | 100 |

**TABLE 5 Marital status by sex**

| Sex | Widowed | Married | Single | Divorced | Sep'd | Total |
|---|---|---|---|---|---|---|
| Male | 75 | 123 | 18 | 5 | 2 | 223 |
| % category | 34 | 55 | 8 | 2 | 100 | 27 |
| % sample | 9 | 15 | 2 | >1 | 1 | |
| Female | 413 | 125 | 62 | 16 | | 617 |
| % category | 67 | 20 | 10 | 3 | | 73 |
| % sample | 49 | 15 | 7 | 2 | | |
| Total | 488 | 248 | 80 | 21 | 2 | 840 |
| % category | 100 | 100 | 100 | 100 | 100 | 100 |
| % sample | 58 | 30 | 10 | 2 | >1 | 100 |

# Age, Sex and Marital Status by Category of Scheme

## Sheltered Housing

The average age of sheltered housing tenants was 78 yrs with little difference between the categories of scheme. Although younger than the residents of Housing-with-Care, there was a significant number of the very old (Table 6).

The distribution by sex and marital status was similar between the three categories of scheme, though rather more of the Category 1 residents were married, 45% vs 28% (Tables 7-8). Of the over 75's in sheltered housing, 80% of the women and 40% of the men were widowed (Appendix 2, Table D). This is a greater proportion than found in the general population.

## Housing-with-Care

The average age of residents of Housing-with-Care was 84 yrs. 74% were over 80 and 53% over 85. Only 9% were under 75 (Table 6).

A high proportion (79%) of the residents were widowed. 25% of all the widowed men were in Housing-with-Care compared with 14.5% of the widowed women (Table 8).

## Guardian

The average age of residents of Guardian schemes was 80.6. There was a very high proportion of over 80's (42% cf 28% in sheltered housing) with 23% under 75 (cf 33%) (Table 6). The highest proportion of women is found in Guardian Housing schemes (82%) which is higher than expected for the age of the residents (Table 7, Appendix 2 Table C). Of the over 75's, 75% of the women and only 1 of the seven men were widowed. This suggests a disproportionate number of widowed women.

## Staying Put

The average age of the clients of the Staying Put project was 71.6 yrs. This is significantly lower than that of the sheltered housing tenants. Just 12% of the Staying Put project were over 80 with 61% under 75 (Table 6).

Clients of Staying Put are the most likely to be married and this category had the lowest proportion of women (66%), reflecting the lower age group population profile (Tables 7-8).

It is the older, single and widowed individuals who move to sheltered housing. Housing-with-Care had the oldest residents and a high proportion of the widowed men. Guardian Housing appeared to attract older widowed women.

**TABLE 6 People in age group by category of scheme (%)**

| Age group | Cat I | Cat I & 2 | Cat 2 | H-w-C | Guardian | Staying Put | Total |
|---|---|---|---|---|---|---|---|
| >70 yrs | 17 | 20 | 7 | 4 | 9 | 39 | 15 |
| 70 — 74 | 21 | 18 | 21 | 5 | 14 | 22 | 18 |
| 75 — 79 | 25 | 28 | 30 | 17 | 25 | 27 | 26 |
| 80 — 84 | 14 | 19 | 21 | 21 | 19 | 10 | 18 |
| 85+ | 23 | 15 | 21 | 53 | 33 | 2 | 23 |
| Total % | 100 | 100 | 100 | 100 | 100 | 100 | 100 |
| Total number | 87 | 190 | 277 | 101 | 78 | 107 | 840 |
| Average age | 77.3 | 76.5 | 78.7 | 84.0 | 80.6 | 71.6 | 77.9 |

**TABLE 7 Sex by category of scheme**

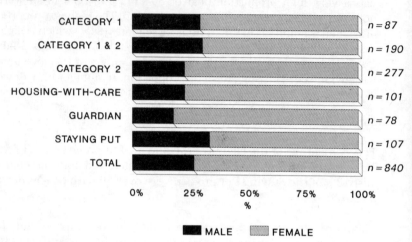

**TABLE 8 Marital status by category of scheme**

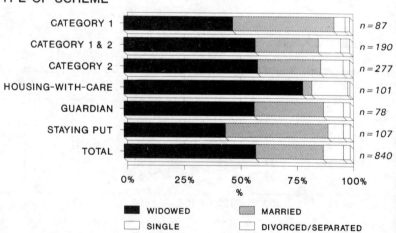

# Household Composition

Who an elderly person lives with is important because it affects their demands on care provision. Married couples are presumed to help one another and as a result be less dependent on the care of others. The older the person, the more likely they are to be widowed and the more likely they are to live alone. There were very few people in the sample who lived with anyone other than a spouse.

92% of Housing-with-Care residents live alone, compared with 66% in sheltered housing schemes and just 44% in the Staying Put project (Table 9). The numbers of people living alone is greater in the schemes with communal facilities (cats, 1&2 and 2).

In the sheltered housing schemes, (excluding Guardian), the numbers living alone does not increase with duration of tenancy at the rate one might expect. The percentage living alone are, for duration of tenancy 1-2 yrs 69%, 3-4 yrs 58%, 5-6 yrs 39%, 7-8 yrs 54%. This implies that increasingly, people who move into Anchor sheltered housing live alone.

**TABLE 9 Who residents live with by category of scheme**

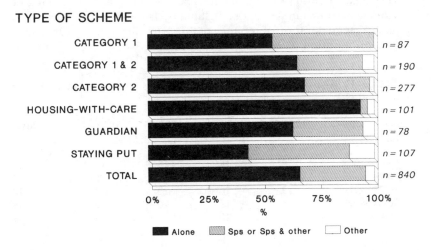

Sps • Spouse

# Age, Age of Schemes and Duration of Tenancy

## Sheltered Housing

The survey looked at age and duration of tenancy to establish whether tenants of Anchor sheltered housing age with the scheme. (Housing-with-Care and Guardian Housing were examined separately.) If tenants did age in this way, old housing schemes could become pockets of high demand on wardens and care services, a criticism which has been levelled at sheltered housing.

The average age of the residents in the oldest schemes is only marginally greater than that of the newer (Table 10). There has been a fairly steady turnover of residents in the older schemes (Appendix 2, Table E). The average age of those resident for 6-8 years is only three years older than those who have most recently moved in. This suggests a steadily increasing age of tenants on moving into Anchor sheltered housing.

Although 52% of the residents of the schemes opened in or before 1976 are 80 years or over, the survey found that there is no consistent pattern to support the view that residents age with their scheme (Table 10).

The mean duration of tenancy in relation to the age of opening of scheme is shown in Appendix 2, Table G. The oldest schemes (1973) have a mean duration of tenancy of 3.1 years, the newest (1986) have a mean duration of tenancy of 1.8 years.

TABLE 10 Age of tenants by year of opening of scheme in sheltered housing (%)

| Age group | 1973-76 | 1979-81 | 1982-85 | 1986-89 | Total |
|---|---|---|---|---|---|
| Under 70 | 9 | 16 | 10 | 17 | 13 |
| 70-74 years | 10 | 20 | 26 | 11 | 20 |
| 75-79 years | 29 | 26 | 29 | 37 | 28 |
| 80-84 years | 24 | 17 | 20 | 9 | 19 |
| 85+ years | 28 | 20 | 14 | 26 | 19 |
| Total % | 100 | 100 | 100 | 100 | 100 |
| Total number | 98 | 231 | 190 | 35 | 554 |
| Average age | 79.8 | 77.3 | 77.1 | 77.7 | 77.7 |

*Housing-with-Care and Guardian Housing*

Housing-with-Care and Guardian Housing are newer schemes, and there are fewer of them, neither show a relationship between age of resident and age of housing.

The mean duration of tenancy in Housing-with-Care, even in the oldest scheme, is only 1.8 yrs. In Guardian Housing the older the scheme the longer the mean duration of tenancy, 2.9 yrs for the 1983 scheme, 2.2 yrs for 1984 and 1 yr for the 1987 scheme (Appendix 2, Table F).

# Dependency and Category of Housing

Having established that Anchor Housing is catering for increasingly older people, who are likely to be widowed and living alone, the survey examined the data on dependency with these trends in mind.

*Sheltered Housing*

The survey found that, surprisingly, there is little difference in dependency between the general population and those in Anchor sheltered housing. 65% of the sheltered housing residents had no disability, 30% some disability and 5% significant disability, the average score was 20 (Table 11a and 11b). This compares with the 1984 Andover research project population[23] of over 75's who had a mean score of 20 with a disability group distribution of 59%, 35% and 6% respectively.

**TABLE IIa Dependency by category of scheme**

TYPE OF SCHEME

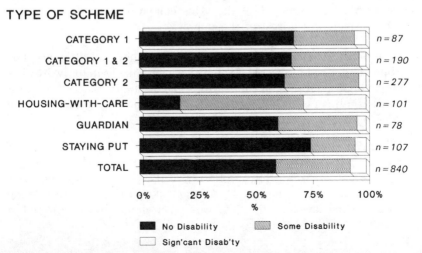

**TABLE IIb Mean score of dependency by category of scheme**

| Disability group | Cat I | Cat I&2 | Cat 2 | H-w-C | Guardian | Staying Put | Total |
|---|---|---|---|---|---|---|---|
| Mean Score | 19.9 | 19.9 | 20.5 | 28.2 | 20.4 | 19.1 | 21.0 |

All the sheltered housing schemes assessed showed a uniformity in the levels of disability; this uniformity is striking, as it differs significantly from the findings in current research in local authority housing in Winchester Health District and a private sheltered housing company. It is probably as a consequence of Anchor's consistent tenant selection policy for Anchor sheltered housing.

It is unlikely that such uniformity would be found in sheltered housing generally without a structured tenant selection policy. The level of dependency found in individual schemes is much more variable in other sheltered housing.

## Housing-with-Care

Housing-with-Care is designed for residents who are in need of the special facilities provided in this type of accommodation. It is aimed at people who do have problems with activities of daily living because of disability or simply the 'frailty' of very old age.

The residents of Housing-with-Care were in fact either disabled or else very old. 28% of residents are in the significant disability group and 55% have some disability. This compares with 5% and 37% respectively in the rest of the sample.

A number of residents (18%) were found to have no disability, but they tended to be very old. 78% of those with no disability were over 80 as opposed to 74% of those with some disability and 71% of those with significant disability. Of the 9 people who were under 75, only one had no disability (Table 18).

## Guardian Housing

Owners of Guardian Housing have already been shown to be older than the average in the sample, and more likely to be female and living alone. Their levels of disability were very similar to those found in Anchor sheltered housing.

## Staying Put

Clients of Staying Put were found to be younger than the average in the sample, (61% are under 75) with very few in the over 80 age group (12% over 80). Despite being younger they had very similar average levels of dependency to the people in sheltered housing. A tendency to display slightly lower disability scores did not reach statistical significance in this sample size. Being younger, they were not necessarily fitter.

# Dependency and Activities of Daily Living

The majority of older people in the survey were shown to be without significant disability, however where difficulties arise with activities of daily living, it is known that the effects on carers and wardens can be out of proportion to the number of people involved.

The disability groups were broken down to examine the nature of disability in the different categories of housing.

## Mobility

The majority of people in the sample could go out independently or with some help, 90% in sheltered housing and 95% in Staying Put. However, in Housing-with-Care only 59% of residents were not housebound.

The questionnaire identifies two categories of being housebound, those able and those unable to manage stairs. The provision of lifts, rather than stairs or someone to help with stairs may determine whether a person becomes housebound or not, and may have an impact on their management.

Housing-with-Care scored the highest overall in this activity of daily living. 32% were housebound (not bed or chairfast) with 28% of residents unable to manage stairs.

In sheltered housing, the total housebound was 9% (not including those bed or chairfast), 12% and 7% and 10% respectively in the Categories 1, 1&2 and 2. and 8% in Guardian housing (Table 12). In all categories, the majority of those housebound were unable to manage stairs.

The number of people who were bed or chairfast in the sample is minimal, the highest category was Housing-with-Care where 9% of residents were bedfast. In Category 1 and Staying Put nobody was bed or chairfast.

**TABLE 12 Mobility by category of scheme (%)**

| Mobility | Cat 1 | Cat 1 & 2 | Cat 2 | H-w-C | Guardian | Staying Put | Total |
|---|---|---|---|---|---|---|---|
| Independent or semi Independent | 88 | 92 | 89 | 59 | 90 | 95 | 87 |
| Housebound | 12 | 7 | 10 | 32 | 8 | 5 | 11 |
| Chair or bedfast | | 1 | 1 | 9 | 2 | | 2 |
| Total % | 100 | 100 | 100 | 100 | 100 | 100 | 100 |
| Total number | 187 | 190 | 277 | 100 | 78 | 107 | 840 |

## Ability to perform personal care tasks

The survey looked at the ability to wash and dress, bathe and go to the toilet unaided. The majority of people in the survey managed all of these tasks unaided. Toilet presented the least problem in all the categories, although it should be remembered that this is a notoriously unreliable question in studies of this nature, for obvious reasons.

Washing presented less difficulty than dressing, it is only in Housing-with-Care that a significant number of residents need any help with either activity, 11% of residents need assistance with washing and 16% need help with dressing. 4% of the residents of sheltered housing needed help with washing with very few needing help with dressing (Tables 13-14).

**TABLE 13 Ability to wash by category of scheme (%)**

| Washing | Cat 1 | Cat 1 & 2 | Cat 2 | H-w-C | Guardian | Staying Put | Total |
|---|---|---|---|---|---|---|---|
| Independent | 94 | 96 | 96 | 89 | 96 | 99 | 95 |
| With Much Difficulty | | 2 | | | | | 1 |
| With Help | 6 | 2 | 4 | 11 | 3 | 1 | 4 |
| Total % | 100 | 100 | 100 | 100 | 100 | 100 | 100 |
| Total number | 87 | 190 | 277 | 100 | 78 | 107 | 100 |

**TABLE 14 Ability to dress and undress by category of scheme (%)**

| Dressing | Cat 1 | Cat 1 & 2 | Cat 2 | H-w-C | Guardian | Staying Put | Total |
|---|---|---|---|---|---|---|---|
| Independent | 99 | 97 | 97 | 85 | 99 | 98 | 96 |
| With Much Difficulty | | | 1 | 1 | | 1 | 1 |
| With Help | 1 | 2 | 3 | 16 | 1 | 1 | 3 |
| Total % | 100 | 100 | 100 | 100 | 100 | 100 | 100 |
| Total number | 87 | 190 | 277 | 101 | 78 | 107 | 840 |

Bathing was more of a problem for older people in all of the categories, especially in Housing-with-Care, where 42% of residents need help and 24% need bathing. In sheltered housing (including Guardian) most people could cope with bathing, 9% needing help or being unable to bath (Table 15).

In summary it is clear that Housing-with-Care caters for the very frail, the majority of its residents are housebound and over a quarter cannot manage stairs. The majority of residents need bathing or help with bathing and a significant proportion are bedfast or need help with personal care tasks.

In sheltered housing only a small proportion of people need assistance with these tasks. However where they do need help, this is likely to make significant demands on the warden, particularly where there is no local authority personal care service. That 1 in 10 cannot bath without assistance identifies a clear service need which may not be being met.

In Housing-with-Care, the requirement for personal care will not remain stable and even slight changes in the number of people needing help will make a big difference in demands for help. This variation could be monitored on a regular basis using either an Activities of Daily Living instrument such as the WDRS or the Beaumont Nursing Dependency Scale[5].

**TABLE 15 Ability to bath by category of scheme (%)**

|  | Cat 1 | Cat 1 & 2 | Cat 2 | H-w-C | Guardian | Staying Put | Total |
|---|---|---|---|---|---|---|---|
| Independent | 93 | 91 | 87 | 33 | 85 | 94 | 83 |
| With Much Difficulty | 1 | 2 | 2 | 2 | 3 | 4 | 2 |
| With Help | 6 | 7 | 11 | 65 | 12 | 2 | 15 |
| Total % | 100 | 100 | 100 | 100 | 100 | 100 | 100 |
| Total number | 87 | 190 | 277 | 101 | 78 | 107 | 840 |

# Dependency, Age of Scheme and Duration of Tenancy

The relationship between age and duration of tenancy was examined in the survey to see whether the oldest schemes housed the oldest tenants. It was found that although the oldest sheltered housing schemes had the highest proportion of over 85 year olds, there was no consistent pattern to support the view that residents age with their schemes. In Guardian Housing and Housing-with-Care, there was no relationship between age and duration of tenancy.

The relationship between dependency and duration of tenancy was examined to see whether the oldest schemes housed the most dependent tenants, and whether duration of tenancy affected dependency.

There is no significant relationship between dependency and duration of tenancy (Table 16) or age of scheme (Appendix 2, Table E), although the two newer Housing-with-Care schemes have higher mean dependency (Appendix 2, Table G).

**TABLE 16a Dependency by duration of tenancy in sheltered housing**

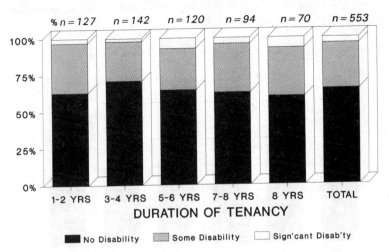

**TABLE 16b Mean score of dependency by duration of tenancy in sheltered housing**

|  | 1-2 yrs | 3-4 yrs | 5-6 yrs | 7-8 yrs | >8 yrs | Total |
|---|---|---|---|---|---|---|
| Mean score | 20 | 19.5 | 20.5 | 20.4 | 21.1 | 20.2 |

# Dependency and Age

The relationship between age groups and dependency was examined to see whether, at any stage, it was possible to say "once an elderly person reaches 80 or 85, (for example) they are much more likely to become very frail and dependent."

This is important to establish because some residents of Housing-with-Care were found to have no disability, but were very old. Do these people really need the facilities of this type of housing merely as a consequence of their age, or are they perhaps being accommodated because their own housing or the alternatives are too demanding? If this is so it would strengthen the case for improved community support rather than more close care accommodation for this type of person.

It was found that there is a significant correlation of age with score in residents aged 74 and over in the Anchor sheltered housing schemes, (R = .35, p = .001). However there is *no* relationship between age and dependency in Housing-with-Care, Guardian Housing on the Staying Put project (Tables 17-20).

**TABLE 17a Dependency by age group in sheltered housing**

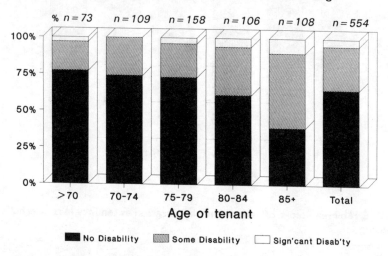

**TABLE 17b Mean score of dependency by age group in sheltered housing.**

|  | >70 yrs | 70-74 yrs | 75-79 yrs | 80-84 yrs | 85+ yrs | Total |
|---|---|---|---|---|---|---|
| Mean score | 18.8 | 18.4 | 19.5 | 20.6 | 23.6 | 20.2 |

**TABLE 18a Dependency by age group in Housing-with-Care**

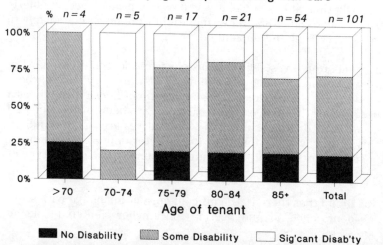

**TABLE 18b Mean score of dependency by age group in Housing-with-Care**

| / | >70 yrs | 70-74 yrs | 75-79 yrs | 80-84 yrs | 85+ yrs | Total |
|---|---|---|---|---|---|---|
| Mean score | 17.6 | 19.4 | 19.9 | 20.7 | 21.8 | 20.4 |

**TABLE 19a Dependency by age group in Guardian Housing**

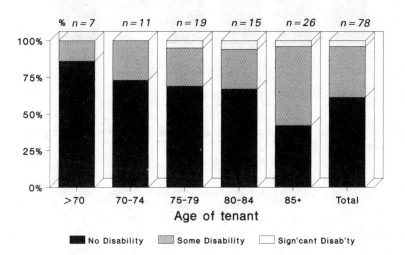

**TABLE 19b Mean score of dependency by age group in Guardian Housing**

| Disability group | >70 yrs | 70-74 yrs | 75-79 yrs | 80-84 yrs | 85+ yrs | Total |
|---|---|---|---|---|---|---|
| Mean score | 17.6 | 19.4 | 19.9 | 20.7 | 21.8 | 20.4 |

**TABLE 20a Dependency by age group in the Staying Put Project**

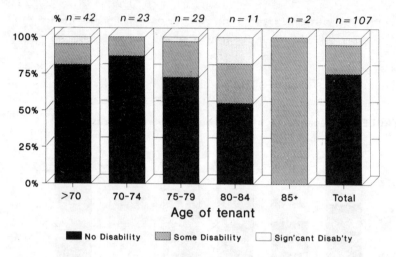

No Disability        Some Disability        Sign'cant Disab'ty

**TABLE 20b Mean score of dependency by age group in the Staying Put Project**

|  | >70 yrs | 70-74 yrs | 75-79 yrs | 80-84 yrs | 85+ yrs | Total |
|---|---|---|---|---|---|---|
| Mean score* | 18.6 | 17.6 | 19.6 | 22 | 22.5 | 19.0 |

* relationship of score with age not statistically significant

# Depression

The depression component of the WDRS-2 was added and validated after the conclusion of the original Andover project, for current research in sheltered housing in Winchester Health District. The validation and results of this study have not yet been published. (See Appendix 1)

The depression component was included in this survey to give an indication of the prevalence of depression in the sample. Although depressive illness may be present in around 25%[6] of the general elderly population, this area has not been addressed in housing for the elderly where it may be especially significant because of the relationship with dependency.

The depression score, being a coarse screening tool, indicates a risk of depression. 75% of those in the risk group will be suffering from depressive illness. Depression increases with dependency and increasing age and women are more likely to suffer from depression than men.

Much depressive illness goes undiagnosed and untreated, although much is amenable to appropriate treatment, particularly when related to unresolved grief. Grieving is associated not only with the loss of loved ones, but also with loss of, or major change in, one's home or life style.

## Risk of depression by age group

The survey examined the relationship between age group and the likelihood of depression in the sample. There is a significant relationship between depression and increased age that is independent of the relationship with increased disability.

**TABLE 21 Risk of depression by age group (%)**

| Risk of deppression | >70 yrs | 70-74 yrs | 75-79 yrs | 80-84 yrs | 85+ yrs | Total |
|---|---|---|---|---|---|---|
| Not depressed | 67 | 68 | 74 | 63 | 64 | 68 |
| 75% risk of depression | 33 | 32 | 26 | 37 | 36 | 32 |
| Total % | 100 | 100 | 100 | 100 | 100 | 100 |
| Total Number | 126 | 148 | 223 | 153 | 190 | 840 |

## Risk of depression by sex

The higher prevalence of depression in women is supported by the findings of this study with 36% of the women and 22% of the men in the '75% risk of depression' group.

**TABLE 22 Risk of depression by sex (%)**

| Risk of depression | Male | Female . | Total |
|---|---|---|---|
| Not depressed | 78 | 64 | 68 |
| 75% risk of depression | 36 | 36 | 32 |
| Total % | 100 | 100 | 100 |
| Total number | 223 | 617 | 840 |
| % of sample | 26 | 73 | 100 |

## Risk of depression and category of scheme

The survey found that age and dependency both varied with category of scheme, and looked at depression to establish whether this also varied by category.

Table 23 shows that a high proportion (42%) of residents of Housing-with-Care are likely to be depressed. There is also a higher than average proportion (36%) of Staying Put clients who are in the depressed group, though this may reflect anxiety rather than depression. It is of particular significance in the light of the lower age of these people. The residents of the sheltered housing and Guardian schemes were similar to the general elderly population with a range from 28% to 33% at risk of depression.

**TABLE 23 Risk of depression by category of scheme (%)**

| Risk of depression | Cat I | Cat I & 2 | Cat 2 | H-w-C | Guardian | Staying Put | Total |
|---|---|---|---|---|---|---|---|
| Not depressed | 72 | 72 | 69 | 58 | 67 | 63 | 68 |
| 75% risk of depression | 28 | 28 | 31 | 42 | 33 | 37 | 32 |
| Total % | 100 | 100 | 100 | 100 | 100 | 100 | 100 |
| Total number | 87 | 190 | 277 | 101 | 78 | 107 | 840 |

# II.                                    Conclusion

The dependency survey has demonstrated that the majority of older people catered for in Anchor housing initiatives, with the exception of Housing-with-Care, have little disability.

All of the sheltered housing schemes measured in the East Pennines region with the WDRS-2 had a uniformly low pattern of disability. Although this may be peculiar to this region, it probably reflects the tenant selection policy of Anchor Housing. Other schemes researched by the authors do not show such uniformity.

In addition the survey has shown that there is no significant relationship between dependency and duration of tenancy or dependency and age of scheme. However some sheltered housing schemes have a significant number of very old tenants, and some significantly disabled people who may put a burden on their wardens out of proportion to their numbers.

Apart from sheltered housing where there was a significant, though weak, relationship between age and dependency in the over 75's, the older people were not necessarily the more dependent.

Housing-with-Care clearly caters for a more dependent population as intended. Those few residents who had low disability scores were very old.

Owners of Guardian Housing tended to be older than residents of sheltered housing and were more likely to be women. They were no less fit than residents of sheltered housing in spite of their greater age.

The clients of the Hull Staying Put scheme were the youngest in the sample group and the most likely to be married. The pattern of disability was the same as for the residents of sheltered housing. Very few over 80's had been helped by the project.

The study looked at the probable prevalence of depression in the sample and found that whilst numbers in sheltered housing were as predicted from general population studies, they were significantly raised in Housing-with-Care and in the Staying Put project. The depression scores in the latter may have indicated anxiety rather than depression.

In conclusion, this report demonstrates that there is no 'time-bomb' of dependency in any of the Anchor sheltered housing schemes in the East Pennines Region. It indicates areas in which Anchor Housing could develop further research, particularly in relation to depression. Worry forms a big part of depression in those living in their own homes and depression influences dependency, this should be considered in both planning housing initiatives and in selection policy for existing housing.

Anchor could look at ways of encouraging elderly people to seek advice on the medical and physical problems they encounter in ageing. Developing a system of dependency surveillance would benefit those people living in their own homes and contacted by Staying Put projects. Out of such a programme a community support service providing assistance with personal activities of daily living could be developed, further reducing the needs that cause old people to move from their own homes.

Anchor should also consider promoting the importance of tenant selection to maintain an appropriate type of admission to sheltered housing, while closely observing the dependency in homes to support wardens.

# 12.

# A Response from Anchor Housing

This study has identified a number of important issues which Anchor will wish to pursue. Some will need further work to be done before firm conclusions can be drawn. The purpose of this section is simply to register the immediate impact of the findings upon us and to offer some thoughts which may lead into further discussion.

The report establishes a very clear difference in the average level of dependency to be found in Anchor's sheltered housing and that present in our Housing-with-Care schemes. All those housed in Housing-with-Care were found to be very old or to present specific features of frailty. This gives endorsement to the effectiveness of Anchor's allocation procedures for Housing-with-Care. It is correctly identifying those who, by these objective measures, need this style of housing and care.

It is obviously important for Anchor to know that it is achieving success in allocating places in Housing-with-Care to those who need them most. This proper concern of good management assumes greater importance when set against the assumption, now widely held, that financial support from the state for those in residential care will, in the not too distant future, depend upon an assessment of their frailty. Anchor recognises the appropriateness of such "gatekeeping" by assessment if limited resources are to be accurately targetted and made available at realistic levels to those who most need them. High quality residential care needs an adequate funding mechanism, part of the process for achieving that must be the more accurate matching of service levels to individual needs.

It is interesting to note that frailty levels among those renting sheltered housing and those purchasing it on leasehold are not markedly different. There has been, in some quarters, an assumption that those purchasing sheltered housing, because their entry depends upon their power to purchase rather than upon an assessment of need, would be a less dependent group. In this study dependency levels appear to be broadly comparable although the average age on entry seems to be higher, as is the proportion of widows.

There are a number of hypotheses which might follow from these findings. It may be that the knowledge that their financial resources allow them to control the timing of their move into sheltered accommodation gives purchasers the confidence to delay their transfer. This is in contrast to prospective renters who must apply early to maximise their chances of allocation. Renters making such an "insurance" application which meets with early success, although subject to assessment, may thus enter sheltered accommodation with much the same level of frailty as the self-selecting group who purchase.

The study finds that there are relatively low levels of dependency among those accommodated in sheltered housing, of whatever category. It is important to recollect that frailty is only one of the characteristics of the applicant which is taken into account in allocating such housing. Questions about the adequacy of the existing housing they occupy, their prospects of finding alternative options and whether their existing situation puts them, in any sense, at risk may all influence the decision to offer sheltered housing.

The finding that length of tenancy does not seem to influence the level of frailty needs careful thought. In the absence of measurements of frailty on entry to sheltered housing in the past one can only speculate about the reasons for this. Anchor believes that it is now receiving tenants who have already reached the levels of frailty that would formerly only have been seen in tenants after several years in sheltered housing.

So far as the clients of Anchor's Staying Put service are concerned the study demonstrates that, whilst on average they are younger than people in sheltered housing their levels of frailty are broadly similar. Does this indicate that poor or unsuitable housing accentuates frailty, or could it be that those experiencing symptoms of frailty are unable to maintain their homes adequately? Clearly there is a connection here between the level of frailty and the need for assistance in achieving repairs, improvements or adaptations to their property. We shall need to look at these results alongside those from the study, jointly commissioned with Care & Repair Ltd, under the title:

"Housing the Essential Element in Community Care", which identified a significant role for these projects in the broader context of community care strategies. The indicators of depression, or possibly of anxiety, in clients of Staying Put is a factor to which we shall wish to return for further investigation.

The researchers report a very striking uniformity of dependency profiles in those sheltered housing schemes studied. This is attributed to the consistency of Anchor's allocation procedures and management practice. An inference which may be drawn from this is that adjustments in policy concerning the characteristics of those allocated to sheltered housing could be implemented in a controlled way. Thus a decision by Anchor to provide sheltered housing to those of a higher level of frailty, with the necessary changes in training and support services for the staff involved, could be implemented with a high degree of confidence in the outcome.

A major area of concern centres around the levels of depression identified by the researchers. The risk of depression was found to be significant among Staying Put clients and highest in residents of Housing with Care. Whilst the researchers believe this feature of their findings to be unsurprising as depression is more likely to be found in women than in men, increases with dependency and increasing age, Anchor must recognise in this a challenge for its patterns of care and support. It is widely recognised that much depressive illness goes unrecognised and untreated. Much of it is amenable to appropriate treatment, particularly when related to unresolved grief. Grief arising not only from the loss of a partner but also loss of a familiar home and lifestyle. Anchor will seek to take account of this area of concern in all aspects of its work and will seek to stimulate further study of this neglected area.

This study has stimulated a number of useful lines of thought and of consideration of our assumptions and our practices within the range of services offered to older people by Anchor. We shall certainly wish to carry forward some of the suggestions for further work to be undertaken. The possibility of repeating this exercise, at least in part, to measure changes over time is one possibility that we shall most definitely wish to pursue.

# Appendix I

## The Winchester Disability Rating Scale

Most activity of daily living questionnaires are designed to record abilities in activities of daily living (ADL) as reported by an observer. A review of instruments for recording dependency showed that most ADL questionnaires are similar, are reliable and easy to use[6]. Many however are long, cumbersome or both.

The Winchester Disability Rating Scale (WDRS) was designed for use in a screening research project. The requirements were that it should record ADL as reported by the person screened, be reliable when used by non-skilled individuals and be rapidly and easily completed.

It is a questionnaire on a single A4 page with 19 questions of which 16 are used to generate a score. It was originally derived from the Rapid Disability Rating Scale-2 (RDRS-2) described by Linn and Linn[7], which demonstrated that an extremely simple ADL questionnaire can be reliable.

The WDRS covers a number of descriptive factors and information on recent hospital admission and recent falls as well as activities of daily living. One question asks specifically how a person feels about their health, a question relates to carers, asked of the carer not the client, and a question on the condition of the home which is the impression of the interviewer. Mental state, anxiety/depression/confusion is covered by only one question because of the desire to reduce the impact of the well documented weakness in relation to simple mental state questions[8].

Scoring is from 1 — 5 for each response. The questions on health and carers are weighted to give added importance to the higher scoring responses. 'Cannot bath' was scored 4 rather than 5.

## Reliability

A pilot of 36 interviews by secretarial and clerical staff at St Paul's Hospital, Winchester, Hants, visiting Day Hospital patients in their own homes demonstrated the reliability of the question structure. The inter and intra-observer agreement on responses to questions of the Winchester Disability Rating Scale is shown below.

| Score Difference | 0 | 1 | 2 | >2 |
|---|---|---|---|---|
| Intra-observer | 83% | 12% | 5% | <1% |
| Inter-observer | 66% | 21% | 12% | <1% |
| Total | 75% | 17% | 8% | <1% |

## Validity

The WDRS score was compared with the CAPE[9] questionnaire score in 41 patients attending the Day Hospital. The Cape questionnaire was completed by the Day Hospital staff and the WDRS completed in the patients' home by a person to whom they were not known.

Comparison of the results from the two questionnaires gave a correlation coefficient of .67 ( $p < .0001$ ). There was a large discrepancy in score in a few individuals which was explained by the difference in viewpoint. One lady who was fairly able in activities of daily living but who was very thin and felt unwell scored well on the CAPE questionnaire but poorly on the WDRS. She was subsequently found to have a gastric carcinoma.

# Use of the questionnaire

In the research project for which it was designed, a change in score of 5 or more points at a visit was a signal for a closer examination of the person to exclude new or changing pathology or physical or social circumstances. It is constructed for use on a micro computer which would permit rapid identification of score changes over few or many assessments.

When all first interviews had been entered into the computer the authors each reviewed 100 questionnaires, divided them into three disability groups and compared results. The score ranges that each had defined were identical but for a very few cases and were therefore adopted. The three groups identified were those with no significant disability (score 15 — 20), those with some disability but whose life is not significantly impaired (score 21 — 33) and those with considerable disability (score > 33).

The time taken for interviews was short, the deciding factor for longer interviews being that the interviewer 'stayed for a chat'. 39% were completed in 1-15 minutes, 38% in 16-30 minutes, 12% in 31-45 minutes, and 11% in over 45 minutes. 17% of all interviews took less than ten minutes to complete.

## WDRS-2

The questionnaire has recently been extended to include items designed to detect depressive illness, the enlarged form being the Winchester Disability Rating Scale — 2 (WDRS-2). This work, carried out with Dr S. Olivieri, Consultant Physchogeriatrician, Winchester Health Authority, is currently being prepared for publication.

# THE WINCHESTER DISABILITY RATING SCALE (2)

SURNAME:               Forename:               Date of Birth:

ADDRESS:

| MARITAL STATUS | Widowed | Married | Single | Divorced/ Separated |
|---|---|---|---|---|

| WHO DO YOU LIVE WITH? | Alone | spouse only | Sp+ other rel | Pt 111 R/Home N/Home |
|---|---|---|---|---|

HOW MANY FALLS WITHIN THE LAST MONTH?

| | | | | | |
|---|---|---|---|---|---|
| 1. WALKING | Independent | Semi-independent | Housebound can manage stairs | Housebound can't manage stairs | Chairfast or bedfast |
| 2. DRESSING/ UNDRESSING | Independent | Some difficulty | Much difficulty | Manages with help | Needs dressing |
| 3. WASHING | Independent | Some difficulty | Much difficulty | Manages with help | Needs washing |
| 4. BATHING | Independent | Some difficulty | Much difficulty | Manages with help | Needs bathing |
| 5. EATING | Independent normal diet | Independent special/ limited diet | Ind. but liquids/ special preps. | Manages with help | Needs feeding |
| 6. SLEEPING | Good nights | Interrupted nights | Poor nights | Awake at night/ asleep by day | Never asleep/ Always asleep |
| 7. TOILET | Independent | Commode at night | Commode day & night | Occasional accidents | Frequent accidents |
| 8. HEADACHES | None | Occasionally | Some of the time | A lot of the time | All of the time |

| 9. HEARING | Satisfactory | Slight impairment | Hard of hearing can lip read | Hard of hearing can't lip read | Totally deaf |
|---|---|---|---|---|---|
| 10. SIGHT | Satisfactory | Some difficulty | Cannot read | Cannot watch television | Blind or almost |
| 11. HEALTH | Good | Good on the whole | Moderate | Poor | Very poor |
| 12. SAD/ WEEPY/ DEPRESSED | Not at all | Occasionally | Some of the time | A lot of the time | All of the time |
| 13. WORRY | Not at all | Occasionally | Some of the time | A lot of the time | All of the time |
| 14. CONFUSION | Not at all | Occasionally | Some of the time | A lot of the time | All of the time |
| 15. COMPANION- SHIP | Good | Some, no more required | Some but more required | Little, no more required | Litle more required |
| 16. PRESENT HELP | None reqd | Some needed & provided | Much needed & provided | More required | Much more required |
| 17. CARER(S) | None reqd | Carer(s) have no difficulty | Carer(s) have some difficulty | Carer(s) under stress | Carer(s) cannot continue |
| 18. HOME/ HOUSING CONDITIONS | Good | Adequate | Inadequate | Untidy or hazardous | Bad |

Completed by                                    date

# Appendix 2

**TABLE A** Age of scheme by category of scheme

| Number of dwellings | Cat I | Cat I & 2 | Cat 2 | Housing-with-Care | Guardian | Total |
|---|---|---|---|---|---|---|
| 1973-1976 | I | | 2 | | | 3 |
| 1979-1981 | 2 | 3 | 4 | | | 9 |
| 1982-1985 | | I | I | I | 2 | 5 |
| 1986-1989 | | | I | 3 | I | 5 |
| Total | 3 | 4 | 8 | 4 | 3 | 22 |

**TABLE B** Size of scheme by category of scheme.

| Number of Dwellings | Cat I | Cat I & 2 | Cat 2 | Housing-with-Care | Guardian | Total |
|---|---|---|---|---|---|---|
| 10-28 dwellings | 2 | I | 2 | I | I | 6 |
| 29-39 dwellings | I | I | 5 | 2 | 2 | 9 |
| 40-79 dwellings | | 2 | I | I | | 7 |
| Total | 3 | 4 | 8 | 4 | 3 | 22 |

The average size of Anchor sheltered housing schemes is 34 dwellings

**TABLE C Number of women by age group in sheltered housing and Guardian Housing**

| Age group | Sheltered Housing | Guardian | Total |
|-----------|------------------|----------|-------|
| Under 70 | 50 (49) | 7 (8) | 57 (12.2) |
| 70-74 years | 73 (67) | 5 (11) | 78 (16.7) |
| 75-79 years | 109 (108) | 16 (17) | 125 (26.7) |
| 80-84 years | 85 (84) | 12 (13) | 97 (20.7) |
| 85+ years | 87 (96) | 24 (15) | 111 (23.7) |
| Total | 404 | 64 | 468 |
| % of Total | 86 | 14 | 100 |

$X^2_4 = 9.8$, $p < .05$

The figure in parenthesis represents the number expected if the age group and scheme were statistically unrelated.

**TABLE D Marital status by sex in sheltered housing.**

| Sex | Widowed | Married | Single | Divorced | Sep'ted | Total |
|-----|---------|---------|--------|----------|---------|-------|
| Male | 36 | 45 | 5 | 3 | 2 | 91 |
| % | 40 | 50 | 5 | 3 | 2 | 100 |
| Female | 216 | 36 | 26 | 3 | | 281 |
| % | 77 | 13 | 9 | 1 | | 100 |
| Total | 252 | 81 | 31 | 6 | 2 | 372 |
| % | 68 | 22 | 8 | 2 | 0.5 | 100 |

**TABLE E Duration of tenancy by year of opening of scheme —
Sheltered Housing (%)**

| Duration of tenancy | 1973-76 | 1979-81 | 1982-85 | 1986-89 | Total |
|---|---|---|---|---|---|
| 1-2 yrs | 24 | 49 | 46 | 8 | 127 |
| (** 75.9) | (25) | (21) | (24) | (23) | (23) |
| 3-4 yrs | 19 | 70 | 27 | 26 | 142 |
| (** 76.9) | (19) | (30) | (14) | (77) | (26) |
| 5-6 yrs | 9 | 28 | 83 | | 120 |
| (** 77.8) | (9) | (12) | (44) | | (22) |
| 7-8 yrs | 24 | 36 | 34 | | 94 |
| (** 78.9) | (25) | (16) | (18) | | (17) |
| +8 yrs | 22 | 48 | | | 70 |
| (** 81.2) | (22) | (21) | | | (12) |
| Total | 98 | 231 | 190 | 34 | 553 |
| % | (100) | (100) | (100) | (100) | (100) |

\* Figures in parentheses=percent.
\*\* Average age

**TABLE F Number of people in each Disability Group by year of opening
of scheme. (%)**

| Disability | 1973-76 | 1979-81 | 1982-85 | 1986-89 | Total |
|---|---|---|---|---|---|
| No Disability | 58 | 155 | 123 | 23 | 359 |
| | /59) | (67) | (65) | (66) | (56) |
| Some Disability | 35 | 67 | 57 | 10 | 169 |
| | (36) | (29) | (30) | (29) | (3) |
| Signif't Disability | 5 | 9 | 10 | 2 | 26 |
| | (5) | (4) | (5) | (5) | (5) |
| Total | 98 | 231 | 190 | 35 | 554 |
| | (100) | (100) | (100) | (100) | (100) |

**TABLE G** Duration of tenancy, average age and mean dependency score by year of opening of scheme.

| Year of Opening | Cat 1, 1&2 and 2 | | | Housing-with-Care | | | Guardian | | |
|---|---|---|---|---|---|---|---|---|---|
| | Mean Dur Ten | Ave Age | Mean WDRS Score | Mean Dur Ten | Ave Age | Mean WDRS Score | Mean Dur Ten | Ave Age | Mean WDRS Score |
| 1973 | 3.1 | 80.4 | 20.6 | | | | | | |
| 1976 | 2.9 | 78.7 | 20.9 | | | | | | |
| 1979 | 2.9 | 80.1 | 20.1 | | | | | | |
| 1980 | 2.9 | 77.3 | 20.3 | | | | | | |
| 1981 | 2.8 | 76.5 | 19.4 | | | | | | |
| 1982 | 2.8 | 77 | 19 | 1.8 | 83 | 27 | | | |
| 1983 | | | | | | | 2.9 | 81 | 21.3 |
| 1984 | 2.4 | 76.4 | 20.7 | | | | 2.2 | 83.4 | 20.1 |
| 1985 | 2.4 | 77.7 | 20.9 | | | | | | |
| 1986 | 1.8 | 77.7 | 20.1 | 1.9 | 83.4 | 24.9 | | | |
| 1987 | | | | | | | 1 | 77.1 | 19.4 |
| 1988 | | | | 1.0 | 83 | 29.2 | | | |
| 1989 | | | | 1.0 | 86 | 28.9 | | | |
| Total | 2.7 | 77.7 | 20.2 | 1.3 | 84 | 28.2 | 2.2 | 80.6 | 20.4 |

**TABLE H** Mean Dependency Score by Scheme.

| | Mean Disability |
|---|---|
| **CATEGORY ONE** | |
| The Gables | 20.5 |
| Flowerlands | 18.8 |
| Flowerbank | 19.6 |
| **CATEGORY ONE AND TWO** | |
| Scholebrook Court | 21.4 |
| Collingwood Court | 19.6 |
| Carlton Fold | 19.0 |
| Muir Court | 20.1 |
| **CATEGORY TWO** | |
| Pembroke Court (1) | 20.7 |
| Brackenhall Court | 20.5 |
| Pembroke Court (2) | 20.9 |
| Peveril Court | 19.7 |
| Chatsworth Court | 20.7 |
| Wadsworth Court | 20.9 |
| Miriam Court | 19.6 |
| Peaselands | 20.1 |
| **HOUSING WITH CARE** | |
| Highfield House | 27.0 |
| Simon Marks Court | 29.1 |
| Heather Vale Court | 29.0 |
| Peaselands | 25.0 |
| **GUARDIAN HOUSING** | |
| Oxenford Court | 21.3 |
| Ireland Crescent | 20.0 |
| Lynwood View | 19.4 |

n=22

# References

1. Surveillance and screening techniques for the elderly. European Health Committee, Council of Europe, Strasbourg, 1988.

2. Carpenter G.I., Demopoulos G.R., Case controlled trial of screening the elderly in the community, in Preventive Care of the elderly: A review of current developments, Occasional Paper 35, Royal College of General Practitioners, London, 1987.

3. Carpenter G.I., Demopoulos G.R., Screening of the elderly in the community: a case controlled trial of dependency surveillance using a questionnaire administered by volunteers. Br. Med. J. 1990, 300, 1253-6.

4. Linton M., Speller V., Carpenter G.I., All of Us — Strategies for health promotion in older people, Wessex Regional Health Authority, Winchester, 1989.

5. Copeland J.R.M. et al., Range of mental illness among the elderly in the community. Prevalence in Liverpool using the GMS/AGECAT package. Br. J. Psychiat. 1987;150:815-823.

6. Phillips D., Assessing dependency in old people homes: Problems of purpose and method. Part 2: Creating dependency Measures. Soc. Serv. Res. 1987;1:30-46.

7. Linn M.W., Linn B.S., The Rapid Disability Rating Scale — 2, J. Am. Ger. Soc. 1982;30:378-382.

8. Williamson J., Lowther C.P., Gray S., The use of health visitors in preventive geriatrics. Geront. Clin. 1966;8:362-9.

9. Pattie A.H., Gilliard C.J., Manual of the Clifton Assessment Procedures for the Elderly (CAPE). 1979, Hodder and Stoughton, Sevenoaks, England.